Peter Alliss GOLF Uncovered

with EDD

MIRTH WARNING

Whilst the hints and tips might well improve your game, and the historical facts will increase your knowledge, never again will a round of golf or a bucket of balls on the range be the same again; every air shot, three putt, draw, fade and skied drive will inevitably force a smile, a giggle or even more!

C O N T E N T S

From Gowff to Golf

It could be said that the game of golf has come a 'fair way' (excuse the pun) since its first chronicled origins in the early 1300s. From being mostly a town game, played towards a target such as a door using a single, lofted iron-headed club, it has moved progressively through the centuries to become the game we know and love today.

You can play, but not on Sunday!

Although banned by successive monarchies during the 1400s, because of its interference with archery practice, golf was soon back on course and gaining royal (*and the archers'*) approval, with King James IV of Scotland buying 'gowff clubbes' from a bowmaker in Perth. Even the Church became involved, with Archbishop John Hamilton, in 1553, declaring that the townspeople of St Andrews would be allowed to play golf on the links of the area. But it was not all plain sailing, according to church records, golfers from Banff to St Andrews were often fined for playing on Sundays 'in tyme of sermonis'. Luckily this was short-lived, in 1603 James I gave royal approval for the enjoyment of the sport on Sundays, providing that golfers had completed their religious duties!

In the late 1600s its popularity in Scotland was growing considerably with both St Andrews and Leith playing a prominent part. In fact the world's first golf club was the Gentlemen Golfers of Leith (later to become The Honourable Company of Edinburgh Golfers), and it was they who, in 1744, drew up the first rules of golf (thirteen of them) to coincide with the first competition for the City of Edinburgh's Silver Club. Other golf clubs soon sprang up imitating their Leith counterparts and became known for their often excessive indulgence in food and drink (*nothing much changes, does it?*).

By the early 1830s recognised leadership of the game had passed to the Society of St Andrews Golfers (formed in 1754), who in 1834 were granted the title of the Royal and Ancient Golf Club of St Andrews. The last quarter of the century brought a dramatic expansion of the game and both North Berwick and St Andrews quickly became popular holiday destinations for the nouveau-riche middle class families who flocked in to play the game. It was during this time that St Andrews witnessed the birth of women's golf as we know it. Meanwhile in America their first club was treated with ridicule. The St Andrews Golf Club of Yonkers, New York was founded by the Apple Tree Gang in 1888 and boasted a three-hole course laid out in the first president's cow pasture.

Thinking about the '*farmyard connection*', did you know that it was not uncommon for golf clubs to own a flock of sheep to keep the fairways down? Although somewhat fluffier than your average greenkeeping staff, they seem to have coped quite adequately but were not allowed on to the greens, which were protected by wire strands. An old-fashioned scythe, similar to a cut-throat razor, was used to cut these and it was the greenkeeper's responsibility to do this by hand. Mind you, given that some courses only had three or four holes, course maintenance couldn't have been that intense, although there were the exceptions whose twenty-two or more holes could have been more than a handful. In fact it wasn't until the 1890s, when golf caught on in England and America, that eighteen holes became the standard for all courses.

Carry your bag, sir?

In Edinburgh and other Scottish towns during the 1700s there were odd-job men, messengers and such, who formed themselves into societies, emulating the gentlemen's clubs of the same period. The members of these societies were called 'caddies', a name said to refer to 'gentlemen freelancers'. Golfing societies and clubs began to hire such men in the late 1700s and the name 'caddie' became part of the game.

Many of the caddies in the early 1800s were also ball-makers and were considered to be 'great judges of the game, and experts at playing it'. Today, little has changed in that respect, although sensibly ball-making is left to the technological professionals. It's hard to believe though that forty-odd years ago the typical 'bag man' boasted a less than perfect background. Apart from the few 'old-school-tie' exceptions, they were an odd-ball selection of layabouts, villains, dropouts and tramps, often more at home sleeping under hedgerows and drinking cider by the quart.

By reputation they were 'wild men living on the fringes of society', wearing the scruffiest of clothes, which they had often slept in. Pedigree and appearance apart however, the noble art was not without its characters.

The Caddie...

Despite exhibiting all the attributes of a pack-mule, the caddie remains dedicated to the human form, and, although not an essential piece of golfing equipment, can prove invaluable to golfers of all abilities. Unlike electric buggies they can only be used to transport clubs, clothing, drinks etc, being unable to support the weight of both player and tour bag simultaneously. Likely to be pushy in matters of club selection and yardage!...

Mad Mac

Picture yourself, if you will, as a spectator in the 50s watching a major tournament. Standing behind the green with a group of spectators you await the approaching group, which includes Max Faulkner, the 1951 British Open Champion.

As they near the green a lone figure breaks away from the group, wild-eyed and resplendent mainly in army surplus gear, with a large pair of lens-less opera glasses hanging from a piece of thick string round his neck. He marches purposefully across the green to where Faulkner's ball is lying and, oblivious to all around, flings himself to the ground behind the ball and peers through the opera glasses to line up the putt. Having established the line he passes on the instructions to Max who dutifully holes the putt.

This eccentric character, known affectionately as Mad Mac, was rumoured to have come from a well-to-do family, with one brother in the Foreign Office and another who was an Air Commodore. True or not? It's not too clear, but what is true is that Mac's on-course eccentricities were reflected off-course as well. One of his most treasured possessions was an old, battered mashie (something like a six iron), bound from neck to grip in rich layers of twine. He would carry this club through London's West End and, if there was not too much traffic about, when he got to Piccadilly Circus he would put a ball down near to Eros and proceed to chip happily down into Leicester Square!

Four under par

Although Max Faulkner's preferred caddie, Mad Mac had another client who looked after him very well. A quiet, reclusive man who passionately enjoyed his round of golf, but preferred to play with imaginary clubs which Mac 'carried' for him. For each hole the fellow would go through the motions – club selection, practice swings, alignment and finally 'hitting' the ball, with Mac dutifully adding the sound effects of the swishing of the club and the crack as it hit the ball! After each shot Mac would hoist the imaginary bag onto his shoulder and they'd walk down the fairway for the next shot.

It was one such day as this when, having reached the 11th, they were caught by the group behind, who were slightly bemused by what was happening. One of the group took Mac to one side to ask what was going on. Mac explained his client's preference for the imaginary, adding that he felt that they shouldn't disturb his concentration due to the fact that he was four under par, which was the best he'd ever achieved on the course.

'What do you mean, four under par?' the man exclaimed in disbelief. 'He's got no clubs, no bag, no ball, what's it all in aid of?'

'To be honest, I'm not sure,' Mac replied in a whisper. 'Not a word to him though! He hasn't got a car either, but he gives me a tenner a week to keep it clean!'

Jaffa

If Mac's eccentricities were behavioural, Jaffa's by contrast were sartorial. Throughout both summer and winter he would wear four (yes four!) overcoats to complement his wellington boots, which were slashed at the side to relieve the pressure on carbuncles which were the size of a fist. At the end of 36 holes on a hot day it was almost possible to see the heat pulsating through rubber of the wellingtons! Once a year, though, he used to strip off (yes *all* of the overcoats) and dive into the canal by Ealing Golf Club and fish out several thousand golf balls (I wonder who looked after the wellies!).

Fairy tales and 'Buckaroos'

It wasn't until the late 50s or early 60s that the regular caddy evolved. In true fairy tale tradition the frog became the handsome prince and an altogether smarter, cleaner, more presentable person appeared. No longer a mere porter but someone who actually *knew* the courses and could be a valuable commodity to both professional and club golfers alike. Forty years on and the professional caddie's role is a respected addition to the modern game.

The characters of today are not nearly as eccentric as their earlier counterparts, although by all accounts there are exceptions, none more so than Buckaroo Banzai. With more hair than Mike 'Fluff' Cowan, Buckaroo is guaranteed to set a few headaches for the R & A should he ever secure a bag on the pro tour. For Buckaroo is a llama, and, according to a site on the Internet, is ideally suited to the role of caddie, as 'golfing is just another form of packing', and apparently packing is what llamas have been developed for – for centuries!

Incredibly strong for their size, they are supposedly great fun to drive, and the structure of their feet, while giving them great agility, will not damage the pristine surface of greens. Training is available for prospective owners on handling techniques, and at least one booklet is available on the subject, apparently written by a golf pro's wife!

Although training is relatively simple, it does require a calm llama and the use of two bags to ensure a balanced load. Can't really see it catching on though!

Who'd be a professional?

It seems hard to believe that, in the early days of golf's growing popularity, a professional's status in the order of things was pretty low. Despite the presence of the now legendary figures of Old Tom Morris (said to be the first salaried professional), his son young Tom, and of course the Park brothers, Willie and Mungo, even successful Open Champions had to tee up the balls of their amateur partners during exhibition matches!

By the turn of the century things began to improve and before long many professional golfers were increasingly becoming recognised as national figures.

However, it was still very rare for the pro to be allowed to enter the clubhouse through the front door. In Britain it wasn't until Henry Cotton was appointed to Ashridge Golf Club in 1937, and was made an honorary member, that the modern day professional's blueprint of acceptance was spawned.

But even so, general acceptance of a pro's 'freedom of the Club' was not uniform and it was not for a good few years that attitudes finally changed and the front doors were flung open wide.

Nothing too seriously wrong! All you need to do is re-align your shoulders and hips, widen and open your stance, check your posture, flex your knees, lift your chin, and your clothes will look great.

... Now let's have a look at the swing!

Aussie rules

Caddies aside, the post-war pro circuit was not without its own club swinging eccentrics, none more so than Norman von Nida, a gritty Australian professional who made few concessions to conformity.

An extrovert in the extreme who, during play, once *demolished* a bunker, believing that he was doing the club, and golf, an enormous favour. The story goes that he was in a deep bunker which had a protruding lip in the direction he wanted to go. After making two or three attempts to get out, with the ball striking the overhang on each occasion and trickling back into the sand, he decided its construction was somewhat unfair and proceeded with his own brand of improvised course maintenance. With his club he methodically chopped away the overhang, hurling the discarded pieces of turf into the bushes to the delight of the Press who were happily snapping away at his mid-tournament antics.

When confronted later by Commander Charles Roe, RN retd, the then Secretary of the PGA, Norman was astonished that anyone should have noticed, let alone taken offence.

'It was unfair,' he protested. 'I was just tidying it up for them!'

On another occasion, one bitterly cold April day at Southport & Ainsdale in the late 40s, Norman donned his trademark onion-seller beret and wrapped himself in a large camel-haired, double-breasted overcoat that swished about his ankles as he marched up to the first tee. At first he took off the coat to play his shots, putting it back on immediately afterwards, but by the time he reached the ninth green it was evident that it was not to be *his* day. His score was in the region of 46 and a drastic change in tactics was needed. The decision was taken, he would keep the coat on *all* the time!

Although it did nothing to improve his score, the sight of Norman's pugnacious, crashing, cavalier-style approach to the closing nine holes, with the voluminous overcoat whizzing round as he followed through, provided an unforgettable spectacle for those lucky enough to be watching. Whilst this cavalier-style approach is still very much part of the modern game, we are indeed fortunate that the camel-haired overcoat never really caught on, although I'm told the beret's trying to make a come back!

Explosive ideas

Sir W.G. (Walter) Simpson, the man credited with the first golf instruction book to feature photos, wrote in the late 1880s about the average golfer's 'armoury':

'Nearly everyone carries a play club (driver), an instrument consisting of many parts. It has no legs, but a shaft instead. It has, however, a toe. Its toe is at the end of its face, close to its nose, which is not on its face. Although it has no body, it has a sole. It has a neck, a head, and clubs have horns. They always have a whipping, but this has nothing to do directly with striking the ball. There is little expression in the face of the club. It is usually wooden; sometimes, however, it has a leather face. Clubs, without being clothed, occasionally have lead buttons, but never any button holes. Clubs' heads are some black, some yellow, but colour is not due to any racial difference.'

If you're any the wiser after this, then you're a better man than I. However, Sir W.G. (would it be presumptuous to call him Walter?) seems to have shown much more promise as an inventor, devising nifty little extras to help prospective golfers sharpen their game. Here are two of the best:

The Automatic Self-Adjusting Tee

A little gadget designed to prevent toeing, heeling, topping, etc, which apparently worked something like the compensating balance of a watch! More impressive still, for convenience you were advised to 'attach the automatic tee to your button-hole by a string which can be used to lift it to your hand after each shot.'

Never really caught on though!

The Dynamite

Eat your heart out, John Daly and the like! This by all accounts was a very powerful weapon. Basically it was a club with a small cartridge inserted in the face, which was designed to explode on contact with the ball, enabling extraordinarily long distances to be achieved.

Not recommended for those with sensitive hearing or anyone with a nervous disposition.

Out of bounds! – Reload!

Clubs at twenty paces

During the 1957 Ryder Cup match at Lindrick, Eric Brown and Tommy Bolt, Scottish and American team members respectively, went missing ten minutes before their starting time. They were discovered on the practice ground, standing twenty paces apart throwing clubs at each other! Fortunately their throwing accuracy, or maybe lack of it, ensured that neither suffered physical injury.

Eric, in fact, was a member of Great Britain's Ryder Cup Team from 1953 to 1959, whilst Tommy played for America in both the 1955 and 1957 teams.

Now Tommy, although a very elegant man, was also quite basic and became quite rebellious when a new rules regime was brought in for the PGA tour in America with fines for all sorts of misdemeanours being implemented. He was in fact once fined $25 for breaking wind on the first tee (*a not uncommon involuntary affliction among club golfers*), claiming that the new restrictions were taking all the 'colour' out of the game, though it was not clear if his playing partners agreed!

However his club throwing antics were legendary and he dismissed many of the great players of the day as 'flippy-wristed college kids', who, he said, were unable to throw their clubs properly! His argument was that they always threw the club in such a way that they had to walk backwards to pick it up. It was said that he once suggested opening a club throwing school so that they could learn to throw clubs, not only in the right direction but at an angle that would not damage the club. I must admit this doubtful skill was one I never felt the need to master!

The Lady Golfer

Much maligned and misunderstood. Demonstrating the ability to play at all levels without the aid of either saucepans, washing machines or dusters. Accepted as a force to be reckoned with both on and off the course.

Capable of driving prodigious distances, but persistently penalised by tee placements being closer to the green than their male contemporaries.

Mary, Queen of Golfers!

I don't know who it was that said, 'a woman's place is in the kitchen, not on a golf course', but I wonder if they realised that the fairer sex's roots in the game date back, possibly, almost as far as those of their male counterparts. Although James IV's royal links with the sport arguably make him the first golfer whose name is known to history.

However, not far behind him comes Mary, Queen of Scots, daughter of another keen golfing king, James V. Born in 1542, she married Lord Darnley in 1565, but eventually the couple were estranged and divorce was discussed. According to rumour an attempt at reconciliation was made and, late on the night of Sunday February 9th 1567, Mary left Darnley's house. Soon after midnight, however, the house was blown up with gunpowder and Darnley's corpse was found in the garden.

So what has this got to do with golf ?

Well, it was alleged that within days afterwards, Mary was seen playing golf at Seton with the Earl of Bothwell, who was suspected of being involved in the murder. According to the records Bothwell was subsequently acquitted of the murder, but poor Mary, alas, was executed. Surely the scores can't have been that bad!

Despite the loss of this important figurehead, ladies golf continued to develop, but it was not until 1867 that the first

women's club was founded, at (*you've guessed it*),
St Andrews. Westward Ho! followed in 1868,
with Musselburgh and Wimbledon founding
clubs in 1872. The Musselburgh fish ladies,
incidentally, had long since been active
golfers, holding an annual Shrove Tuesday
match where the 'marrieds' reputably always
beat the 'unmarrieds' – or should that be the
'missuses' always beat the 'misses'?

Carnoustie's women's club was founded
in 1873, followed by Pau in France, in
1874. Unfortunately emancipation was
a long way off and playing facilities
within these clubs were restricted. 'Ladies links', it was written by Lord
Wellwood in *Badminton Golf*, 'should be laid out on a smaller scale of
the long round, containing some short holes and some long holes,
admitting a drive or two of 70 or 80 yards.' He went on to say that,
'the postures and gestures requisite for a full swing are not
particularly graceful when the player is clad in female dress'. A
sentiment obviously shared by a Miss A. M. Steward who wrote, in *The
Gentlewomen's Book of Sports*, that 'a damsel with even one modest
putter in hand was labelled a fast and almost disreputable person'.

The ladies, obviously not disheartened by all this negative attention,
continued to persevere with their devotion to the sport. St Andrews
Ladies' club, in fact, had attracted over 500 members, but the one
thing lacking overall was a single championship to test their skills. So in
April 1883 the LGU was formed, and, by June 1883, thirty-five eager
ladies contested the first Women's Amateur championship at Royal
Lytham and St Anne's. It was won by Lady Margaret Scott, an eighteen-

year-old Gloucestershire lass whose skills far exceeded her nearest rivals, and, to the great satisfaction of the LGU committee, 'photographed extremely well'.

Sartorially, 'smart but casual' was not the order of the day and you can only marvel at their ability to play in what was generally accepted as correct female golfing attire. With a look more associated with Mary Poppins, the outfit comprised: stockings, chemise, boned corset, garters, drawers, two petticoats, a long sleeved blouse with fitted cuffs, a long skirt, boater and gloves!

Male sceptics, obviously influenced by both the quantity of clothing and the perceived lack of grace, poured scorn on the championship suggesting it would be the 'first and last', adding that it was inconceivable that ladies, being 'unfitted for golf', could last through two rounds of golf in one day.

How wrong they were!

Ladies only

Britain boasts two 'Ladies only' golf clubs, one having already celebrated its Centenary and the other with three more years to go.

Formby Ladies, Formby, Liverpool was founded in 1896 and still has a thriving membership. Highly admired for its 'smart but casual' approach, it has become a favourite venue for not only ladies, but men's golfing societies who return time after time, not just for the golf, but for the homemade cakes and the outstanding hospitality.

Sunningdale Ladies, founded in 1902, has a membership of 400 and enjoys a more private profile, but men are allowed to play on the course.

What's yours called?

Dorothy Campbell, a self taught Scottish golfer, completed the double in 1909 by winning the British Women's Amateur Championship, beating Florence Hezlet, and then travelling to Pennsylvania to beat Nonna Barlow for the American title, never being taken past the 17th hole throughout the championship.

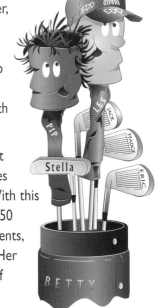

Her clubs were her friends, to the extent that she gave them all names. One of her favourites was a goose-neck five-iron called 'Thomas'. With this club she could always get up and down from 50 yards and, much to the distress of her opponents, occasionally holed a run-up of that distance. Her putter, another favourite, enjoyed the name of 'Stella' and starred in many of her matches.

Edd says the closest he can get to this is a putter called Ping. Hasn't got the same kind of magic, has it?

A stone's throw away

During the campaign for women's suffrage, countless greens were damaged and numerous windows were broken at clubs, because many suffragettes believed that the 'Golf Club' was a bastion of male domination.

Picture then the scene at Woking Golf Club, around 1910, when lady members were merely temporary members with a different title. Ethel Smyth, a 'lady member', composer, writer and a close friend of Emily Pankhurst, the founder of the Suffragette movement, has invited Emily to join her at the course.

On arrival they march off towards the 13th fairway holding between them what appears to be a bulging carpet bag. Ethel leads the way with her dog and Emily Pankhurst following behind. Reaching what appears to be the mid point of the fairway they stop and tip the contents of the bag on to the ground. There in front of them is a pile of well rounded stones which they proceed to throw along the fairway.

Whether or not this was a breach of local rules is not certain, but judging by Emily's first throw, which nearly hit Ethel's dog, the practice was sorely needed!

Mix and match

By 1910 the ladies golfing 'uniform' became more
relaxed, with several layers being discarded.
However, what was lacking in clothing, was
more than compensated for by the abundance
of names the ladies enjoyed, none more so
than Charlotte Cecilia Pitcairn Leitch.

Known as Cecil Leitch to her friends, she played golf to a very high
standard and took on Harold Hilton, a former Open winner, in a
challenge match played over 72 holes, with 36 holes at Walton Heath
and 36 holes at Sunningdale.

Played off the men's tees, the match required Harold to give half a
stroke per hole to Cecil, who started nervously but was only one
down after the first 36. At Sunningdale Cecil won on the 71st hole,
taking only 77 strokes for the final 17 holes, while Harold's 75 were
not enough to prevent defeat.

What train?

In 1920 Joyce Wethered won her first English Women's Amateur title,
beating defending champion Cecil Leitch. Joyce, not yet 20, holed the
winning putt on the 17th hole from eight feet, despite a train rattling
past just a few yards away.

When asked if the noise of the train had disturbed her concentration.
She looked puzzled and
asked, 'What train?'

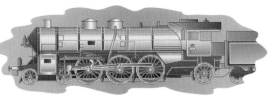

From then on the
hole was known by
that name.

We won't peep, honest!

Ethel Smyth, the famed stone-throwing suffragette and still 'temporary member' of Woking Golf Club, was the shock recipient of the title of Dame of the British Empire in the New Year's Honours List of 1923. It came as a surprise to everyone apart from Ethel who was convinced it was the outcome of her friendship with Lord Riddell, the lawyer and newspaper proprietor who was also a member of Woking Golf Club.

It seems that his lordship was aware of Ethel's stirling troubleshooting in a dispute between the men's and women's sections. Apparently a quantity of women members had been regularly taking a short cut between the general club rooms and the women's section. The route which they took led directly past the men's changing rooms and the men were less than pleased. In fact rumour had it that there was a possibility of a weekend ban on women's golf.

At a Ladies' committee meeting she pointed out that there was no doubt that, 'given the modesty of the British male', their chief crime lay in taking the short cut. After much hilarity, the 'short-cutters' voted almost unanimously to abandon the route and compromised male dignity was restored to its former 'glory'.

Well done Ethel!

I'm sure a lot of Ladies' Sections nowadays would still welcome the 'street-wise' diplomacy and negotiation skills of Ethel within their club environment, though they might draw the line at her stone throwing!

Clubhouse Tales

From the depths of the undergrowth to the middle of the trees, from the centre of the fairway to the heart of the green, the endless battle against the elements goes on and on.

Meanwhile, back at the Clubhouse ...

It's in the bag!

Years ago there was a regular at Altrincham Golf Course who would turn up to play carrying a small compact golf bag with a large, floppy zipped pocket on the side. After eighteen holes, Hugh Lewis the club pro couldn't help noticing that this hitherto floppy pocket was visibly bulging and that its owner was obviously finding the bag more difficult to carry.

After several rounds, Hugh was becoming more and more curious, and more than a little concerned, about the pocket's mysterious contents. Although nothing or no one had been reported missing he felt he ought to know. Finally, curiosity got the better of him. He went over to the man and tactfully said,

PLEASE
REPLACE
YOUR
DIVOTS

'You seem to be stuffing an awful lot of stuff into that pocket. It doesn't do the zip any good, you know!'

The bag's owner replied with a grunt and a nod, turned and walked off towards his car. Hugh, however, determined to press the point, caught up with him and asked to see inside the pocket. Sheepishly the chap slowly opened the zip to reveal that the pocket was crammed full with big divots.

'What the hell do you think you're doing with these?' Hugh asked in amazement, 'You know you should always replace your divots!'

'I know,' said the chap. 'I *always* put my own divots back, but these are ones that other people haven't. You see, I've got this little garden at home and I'm making a lawn, so I take these divots home while they're damp and re-lay them. I get almost a square metre every time I play!'

The Greenkeeper

EDD © 1997

At one with nature, the unsung hero of the course, with commando-like survival skills, avoiding committee and member confrontation with consummate ease, whilst inflicting maximum disruption and discomfort for the 'good of the course'! Rarely thanked, often criticised, but never wrong!

(... so they tell us! ...)

27

Dead on target

During one of the Pro-Celebrity television series at Gleneagles, Lee Trevino paused before his tee shot to tell the story of two golfers who, for a change, agreed to go round the course using their imaginations instead of golf balls.

The first player drove off, 230 yards straight down the middle of the fairway. The second man hit an equally good drive, his ball ending four feet ahead of his opponent's. It was nip and tuck all the way round and they arrived at the 18th with their scores even.

Off the 18th tee they both played good drives and the first player had first crack at the green. After a moments thought, he pulled out a four iron and hit an absolute peach which never left the flag, landing on the green and hopping forward straight into the hole.

'It's in! It's in!' he shouted, leaping about excitedly.

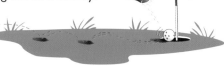

'Damn, so it is,' his opponent replied, adding, 'But you played the wrong ball!'

In ... out, change it all about!

The late Ben Sayers, great player and clubmaker from North Berwick, was said to have sold two right-handed and two left-handed clubs to a rather over-bearing American who felt that the game of golf was rather beneath him.

Several hours later the American returned, confronting Sayers and complaining bitterly that he had been made a fool of. Quick as a flash,

Ben Sayers authoritatively replied to the American's complaint.

'It's quite in order, sir,' he said, 'What you do is use the right-handed clubs for the holes going out and then use the left-handed ones coming in.'

Left, right; left, right ...

It's often very difficult when you take up a sport to establish your needs, especially when you adopt the do-it-yourself approach without the benefit of professional advice and expertise. An example of this is a story which originates from the pro shop at the Roundhay Municipal Course, Leeds.

Two chaps turned up one day straight from work. The first, who had his own clubs and looked the part, paid his green fee and explained that his mate also wanted a game but would need to hire some clubs.

'Right or left-handed?' asked the pro.

'I don't know yet,' said the other man. 'I haven't played before, give us a few of both!'

An Aladdin's cave of should haves, must haves and wanna haves. A tingle of excitement and anticipation every visit.

'Now let's see, what colour tees shall I buy today?...'

Where's the putter?

John Stirling, one time professional at Meyrick Park, Bournemouth, used to take evening classes at the local church hall using plastic Airflow balls. With him he would take a golf bag filled with seven irons, that his pupils would use. After the class he would take them back to the pro shop and store them away.

One cold winter's evening after the class, he returned to the shop, opened the door and forgetting it was his day off the next day, pushed them inside ready to put away in the morning.

The next day on visiting the shop to pick up his cheque book, he was pleased to discover that business had been quite brisk and that all 22 sets of hire clubs were out. Whilst John was pleased to hear that the shop was thriving, he was somewhat confused over the hire clubs as only 21 sets were available.

However 22 sets had been logged in the book. Suddenly it clicked, the 22nd set just had to contain the 21 seven irons which he used for coaching. With a mixture of embarrassment and stifled giggles he turned to his assistant to pull his leg, but, before he could say anything, the man who had hired the clubs walked in to the shop.

'Did you enjoy your game, sir?' he said, expecting a severe tongue lashing.

'Yes thanks,' replied the man, adding, 'You know I've only been playing for six months, but that's the best set of clubs I've used. Next time though, can you put in one of those flat clubs like the pros use on the telly, cos it was a little tricky on the greens!'

Noddy hidden!

In these days of sexual awareness and the general
acceptance that safe sex is best, it seems hard to
believe that something as common-place today as the
simple 'French letter' (or condom to the uninitiated)
could have been the source of cold chills down the
spine during my professional playing days.

Hugh Lewis and I, and one or two others, became involved in
Lewis's devious, wicked and very funny creation, which centred on these
harmless protective sheaths, code-named 'Noddies' (*apologies to Enid
Blyton!*). The idea was that, during a function, tournament or gathering,
the cry of 'Noddy hidden' would go up, meaning that one these soon to
be dreaded items had been hidden in a way likely to cause great
embarrassment to the targeted finder.

Time passed by and more ingenious hiding places were found. As well-
known players stepped up to the first tee, a whispered 'Noddy hidden'
warned of impending embarrassment as they pulled off their head
covers and discovered, too late, the packet of three as it floated to the
ground for all to see. Nowhere and no one was safe, 'Noddies' were
hidden behind sun visors in cars, wrapped up in waterproofs
and even stretched over driver heads, with the customary
'Noddy hidden' warning timed to perfection for maximum
panic generation. Putting up an umbrella was a nightmare
and believe it or not on one occasion they even stretched
one over the handle of a friend's Hoover. Being
transparent, it was days before his poor wife noticed, and
in the meantime those responsible giggled like naughty
schoolboys at the thought of this poor lady making innocent
hand movements up and down the handle of the cleaner
as she banished the dust with firm, brisk strokes!

Finally, after yours truly had been 'Noddied' on the first tee of a tournament, when a 'Noddy' fell out of my glove, I decided it was time to get my own back.

Soon the opportunity arose and while I was staying at Hugh Lewis's house, a drinks party was arranged. Several hours before the party I got one of the ice trays out of the fridge, put a 'Noddy' in one of the compartments, filled the tray with water and slipped it back into the freezer compartment.

With the party at full swing and Hugh socialising with the guests, the moment had arrived. Having offered to get Hugh a refill, I went into the kitchen, poured the gin, added three ice cubes (the 'Noddied' one at the bottom) and topped it with a generous slice of lemon.

After pouring myself a drink, I rejoined the party, walked over to Hugh's group and handed him his drink. Hugh accepted it with a charming smile and carried on chatting. I watched with quiet satisfaction as the heat of his hand warmed the glass and the ice started to melt.

Timing it to perfection, I waited until the top two cubes had virtually disappeared and the third was ready to reveal its secret.

'Noddy hidden!' I whispered in his ear.

At that very moment the offending article surfaced and 'Noddy' wasn't hidden any more. Hugh's face was a picture, with a mixture of horror and embarrassment he beat a hasty retreat, hoping that nobody had noticed. Wishful thinking unfortunately, it became quite a talking point, not only for the rest of the party and for a good while afterwards. But from that day onwards 'Noddy' remained hidden, apart of course from when he went out with Big Ears!

It's not the winning,
.... it's the taking part!

Another one of those if-only rounds! Out in 34 and even par for the next four holes; then top, sky, shank, push, pull, hook, slice, two four-putts, two out-of-bounds, three in the water and an air shot – back in 72! ...

Perhaps I'll get my handicap cut next time!

It can't get any worse!

At Arcot Hall in Northumberland, not far from the clubhouse, in fact by the side of the ninth green, there used to be a lake. It is said that one day, after one of those 'it can't get any worse' rounds, a disillusioned member was seen to approach the lake, raise his bag of clubs above his head and throw it in, watch it disappear under the water and then return to the clubhouse.

After a few stiff whiskies, taken alone at the bar, he got up and marched back outside and approached the lake. Taking off his shoes and socks, he rolled his trousers up to his knees and waded into the water. Rolling up his sleeves he reached down, recovered his bag and carried it back to the bank, where he laid it down beside his shoes.

Having put his shoes and socks back on he reached towards the bag and unzipped one of the pockets, put his hand inside, took out his car keys, then threw the bag back into the lake and was never seen at the club again.

Hidden relief

The scene is the Walker Cup Dinner at Turnberry in 1963. An American team member was asked how one of his compatriots was playing back home.

After a bit of thought he said, 'He's just about given up the game, of course he was never basically sound – his grip was all wrong. It reminded me of a man trying to relieve himself behind a tree without anybody seeing!'

Just thought I'd let you know

At Croham Hurst Golf Club, near Croydon, one of the members had been very unwell with what was eventually diagnosed as heart trouble. After being hospitalised for treatment he was fitted with a pacemaker. On returning home he felt so much better, in fact his sex life *and* his golf improved dramatically. With his new found enthusiasm and stamina he started to play more and more golf and was very proud of his progress.

One weekday he turned up at the club and found a visitor looking for a game. Introductions completed they walked over to the first tee and the member couldn't resist telling his story. With great pride in his voice he declared,

'I've got a Pacemaker!'

'I'm playing a Titleist 3,' replied the visitor.

Half an inch off the left one!

In the 30s, Pilot-Officer Douglas Bader lost both his legs in a terrible crash at Woodley Aerodrome, near Reading. At Roehampton Hospital he was fitted with metal legs, and with grit and determination he learnt to walk again, drive a car and even fly a plane.

One day, while still wobbly on his new legs, a friend offered him a 7-iron and he tried to hit a golf ball. Falling over twelve times before he made contact he had to drastically reassess his swing. With a much slower, and considerably less dramatic approach he succeeded in both striking the ball *and* staying on his feet. From then on golf became an obsession and, practising at the North Hants Club, he exercised his steely determination, fine eye and muscle co-ordination, until at last he was able to play a few holes. Three, six, nine and finally eighteen. Quickly his scores dropped to under 100.

When his handicap had reached 18 and he was playing frequently in competitions, news of his exploits reached Henry Longhurst, then one of our most distinguished amateurs. Longhurst travelled down to North Hants and was amazed when Bader went round in 81. During the many times they played together, Henry noticed that Bader's second shot, on the 5th, where the fairway sloped gently up to the green, was always particularly well struck. He decided that the uphill lie made it easier for Bader to get squarely behind the ball and at the same time helped the resistance down his left side as he struck the ball and followed through. On discussion they decided that it would be an ingenious move to trim half an inch of one leg to duplicate the same effect on level ground.

Longhurst Stance Development

Previously Bader had persuaded Roehampton to fit a universal joint to each ankle to increase mobility. Now, excited by the prospect of better golf, he put the new suggestion. Eventually they agreed and the appropriate adjustment was made. Sure enough his game seemed to immediately benefit from it and when the news reached Henry, he wrote an article for the Evening Standard about the man who had removed half an inch from his left leg in order to play golf with a permanent uphill lie. On seeing the article, Bader rang Henry excitedly.

'You silly goat,' he said, 'I had it taken off my *right* leg, not the left one!'

'Good God,' said Henry in amazement, 'you've had it taken off the wrong leg!'

Texas Scramble

A team competition known to have many regional and global variations, which, despite its title and shotgun start, does not insist that participants are either oil barons, rodeo riders, cattle ranchers or cowboys!

Scramble: Make way as best as one can over steep or rough ground by clambering or crawling etc!

Red Alert

Golf pros are sometimes accused of not having much of a sense of humour. A completely untrue story of four pros – myself, Dai Rees, Christy O'Connor and Eric Brown – has us playing an exhibition match in Aberdeen at the time of a blow-out at one of the oil rigs. We were sitting in the Station Hotel in Aberdeen having a drink. when I looked up and saw a group of characters in stetsons and cowboy boots at the bar, and said knowingly to the assembled company:

'That's Red Adair!'

Eric Brown shook his head in disbelief and despite my assurance was not convinced that my observation was accurate. In an attempt to prove his point he walked over to the bar and confronted the stetson clad group. After a brief exchange of drinks and a lively conversation he returned to our table, grudgingly agreeing that it really was the great man.

Dai Rees, however, was not convinced. Shaking his head he marched over to the bar to interrogate the men in cowboy boots. Once again, after a brief exchange of drinks and a lively conversation he returned to our table confirming the famous Texan's identity.

In true Englishman, Scotsman, Welshman, Irishman tradition the inevitable happened and Christy O'Connor sprang to his feet still doubting the truth:

'I still can't believe that's Red Adair!' he said as he walked towards the stool on which the Texan was perched. He looked into the great man's eyes and said:

'Excuse me, sorr, I'm sorry to be interrupting you again, but my friends tell me you're this great man Red Adair.'

Red by this time was feeling quite flushed from more than enough bourbon, but was obviously quite pleased with all the adulation.

'Yeah, you're quite right, boy. Like I told your friends, I sure am Red Adair.'

Christy smiled, shuffled his feet rhythmically and said in that light soft Irish brogue:

'Tell me, what was it really like dancing with Ginger Rogers?'

Worth its weight in gold

Playing in the 'Dad's Army' section of his local club, Harold never ceased to be surprised by the antics of his playing partner, George.

Week after week, round after round, George would chase after his ball with reckless abandon, following his misdirected shots like a man on a mission. In the trees, in the bushes, in the brambles, in the water and even out of bounds until the ball was found.

It was not as if his scores warranted such dedication. Harold's frustration at not knowing why finally reached a peak and he felt duty bound to ask the question.

'Look here George,' he said, 'every time you hit your ball into the bushes or hook it over the road, in the trees or out of bounds, you insist on chasing after it. Why?'

With a pained look George replied, 'It's my lucky ball!'

Always keep your eye on the ball!....

'Take no prisoners!'...

The motto of the intrepid band of men known in golfing circles as "Dad's Army". Armed with vitamin supplements and the odd bottle of Grecian 2000, they march doggedly along the fairways, through the deepest undergrowth and ever onward to the greens, often in zig-zag formation with a military precision fading with the passing years. Understated achievers to the man, their success is limited only by their stamina and creaking joints.

EDD © 1999

The Electric Trolley

A useful addition to the golfer's armoury.
Once considered a luxury and more readily
associated with those of ascending years,
the electric trolley has gone from strength
to strength and is now seen at all levels of
golf. Not recognised by any of the major
breakdown organisations, they can be
prone to erratic, and often uncontrollable
performance when used near electricity
pylons and mobile phones!

EDD © 1999

Fore left!!...

At one of our better-known clubs, the third hole runs parallel with the busy main road. During a medal round, a player hooked his tee shot and shattered the windscreen of a passing double-decker bus. The bus swerved and crashed into an approaching lorry. In an effort to avoid the bus and lorry, several cars in each direction crashed into each other and two cyclists and several pedestrians were injured. Within minutes the scene was like a battlefield.

Several ambulances, fire engines and police cars soon arrived and the golfers, somewhat red-faced and concerned by the severity of the accident, made their way through a gate leading on to the road to see if they could help.

On reaching the scene they were confronted by a senior policeman who said:

'Which one of you is responsible for this carnage!'

One of the group stepped forward rather sheepishly. 'I'm afraid it was me,' he said.

The policeman looked at him, as only policemen can, and asked forcefully, 'What are you going to do about it then?'

The golfer blushed and, still shocked by everything that had happened, took a moment to think before he replied.

'It must be grip that's wrong,' he said thoughtfully, 'What I need to do is get my right hand further round the shaft!'

Good shot

Isn't it funny how at every championship or tournament there is always that lone voice whose often ill-timed and misdirected cries of: 'You're the man!', 'Good shot!' or 'Way to go!' separates them from the crowd. Fuelled by the belief that that their vocal encouragement can really give their idols the winning edge, they faithfully follow their chosen group for the full eighteen holes, or more, satisfied that their invaluable contribution has been noticed.

Nothing much changes you know, for in my younger days I was sitting with my father in his shop at Ferndown when suddenly the door burst open and a man walked purposefully in. Throwing up his arms he walked towards my father and, grinning from ear to ear, called my father's name as if he was greeting a long lost friend.

My father looked up over the top of his glasses and said, 'Good morning.'

'Percy, Percy, Percy, don't you remember me?' asked the man enthusiastically.

Dad stared blankly back at him, trying frantically to remember. 'I'm sorry!' he said apologetically.

Quick as a flash the chap whipped off his cap and, still grinning, he asked, 'Now do you know me?'

Poor Dad still couldn't summon the faintest spark of recognition, even when the man took off his glasses it still meant nothing. The visitor couldn't hide his disappointment, he was beside himself.

'Don't you remember the Ryder Cup matches at Southport & Ainsdale in 1929?' he asked.

'Yes, of course I do!'

'So you must remember your match with Gene Sarazen, then?'

'Of course I do,' said father.

The man continued, 'You know at the second hole you pulled your tee shot just to the left side of the fairway and, although your ball was on the fairway, you were standing about six or seven inches above it.'

Pausing only to see my father nod as if in agreement, he continued, 'Then you played the most incredible shot which pitched just short of the green and finished eight foot from the pin.'

'Yes, yes I remember,' father said. 'But I still don't ...'

Before he could finish the man interrupted, proclaiming proudly, 'Well, I was the fellow who shouted "Good Shot"!'

Pancake golf

Before finishing the 18th hole, Harry broke away from his fourball and ran towards the clubhouse clutching his golf towel to his head, in an attempt to stem the flow of blood from a gaping wound above his ear. A fellow member rushed over to help him, asking:

'What on earth happened to you, are you all right?'

Harry, by now feeling a bit weak, sat down on the wall by the practice green and murmured, 'It was horrible, quite horrible!' and then he fainted.

By the time the paramedics left he was feeling a little better and was able to explain what had happened.

'I was playing in a mixed greensomes with my wife and we had reached the 18th,' he said. 'My opponent's wife sliced her tee shot into the cow pasture that runs down the side and she was rather upset about the thought of losing her favourite ball, so all four of us went to look for it,' he continued, pausing only to take a sip of the 'medicinal' brandy that had been placed in his hand.

After a cough for sympathy, he went on, 'Anyway, after a long search we couldn't find it, and by now the poor woman was really upset, so I decided that there was only one thing left to do.'

'Yes, yes?' said his friend who was hanging on every word. 'So what did you do?'

'In what must have been a rush of blood to the head, if you'll excuse the pun, I went round to each of the cows and lifted their tails in turn. Suddenly, there it was, just barely visible!' he paused for another medicinal sip, 'So in my excitement I called over my opponent's wife and, holding the cows tail out of the way, I pointed to the spot saying, "Does yours look like this?" and she hit me with her five iron!'

In the clear

Rumour has it that the TV companies will do anything to improve their coverage. A story of doubtful origin revolves around the Open Championship coverage by ABC Television at St Andrews in 1970. The story goes that they sent a scouting party ahead to determine the best places to locate their cameras etc.

One of the party, somewhat of an opportunist, put in a bill to the Company, for a considerable amount of money. The bill was itemised and amongst the things listed it quoted large amounts for tree clearing, branch cutting and the like in order to place cameras in the optimum positions. (Hands up those of you who don't remember trees there).

Anyway, it just so happened that the Chief Executive of ABC was over in Scotland just after the Championship and while there, he visited St Andrews.

On returning to the head office in New York, he called the opportunist in and confronted him.

'You charged us an awful lot of money for tree clearing, before the Open Championship, he said. 'I've just returned from St Andrews, there's not a tree in sight!'

'So you can see what a good job I did!' said the fellow, his fingers crossed firmly behind his back.

The 'cut' shot!...

A must for 'slicers'! Played exclusively with the rarely seen scythe iron, featuring an enlarged sweet spot on an extended razor sharp blade. Perfect for all those tricky shots out of thick rough, dense undergrowth and trees. Complicated only by the size and dangerous nature of the club.

Only recommended for trolley-pulling or buggy-driving golfers!

Train spotting

HURRY UP
AND FINISH
YOUR ROUND!
THE LAST
TRAIN FOR
EDINBURGH
LEAVES IN
15 MINUTES!

You might have noticed how many golf courses are close to both railway lines and stations. Back in the 1920s, when the motor car was still in its infancy and the M25 was not even a twinkle in someone's eye, the preferred form of transport to the golf club was often a train.

The only trouble with trains was that, unlike taxis, they didn't come when you whistled for them. In order to reach some of the more desirable links courses to the east of Edinburgh, members often had to wait half an hour, or more, at a small junction a couple of miles from the course.

Imagine the scene, one cold, wet March afternoon. The platform is deserted apart from two men, isolated only by the rain which falls between them. No shelter in the sight and the train is already half an hour late. Exasperated and unable to bear the silence any longer, one of the men walks up to the other and, although they haven't been introduced, gestures across the fields in the direction of the course.

'Dammit,' he says, 'I've been a member over there for thirty years and I reckon I've spent eight months of that at this station!'

I think I'll stick to my car!

Incidentally, talking about trains, it was once said that Harry Vardon, on an off-day, asked his caddie's advice on course management,

'What on earth shall I take now?' he enquired.

To which his caddie replied, 'Well sir, I'd recommend the 4.05 train!'

Enough said!

It's in the water!...

When faced with the mind numbing decision of whether to play the 'watered' ball, adopt the French relaxation technique of rolling up your trousers, removing your shoes and socks, and paddling.

With feet suitably refreshed, you'll feel completely relaxed and find it easy to decide where to drop the ball!

Anyone seen my ball?

Tommy Horton,, currently enjoying considerable success on the Senior Tour, told me a rather good story about a mad-keen golfer called Henrik Lund. Now Henrik, a qualified lawyer, just used to turn up at tournaments all over the world. A delightful eccentric who was more than likely to turn up wearing four roll-neck sweaters and an overcoat, at even the hottest of venues.

During one of these 'impromptu' appearances at the Italian Open, held at the Pevero Course on the east coast of Sardinia, it was early morning and the temperature was bitterly cold. Henrik was first out for a threeball with David Russell and Tony Charnley.

Now Pevero is a wonderful course, but very hard, being landscaped through rock. There are great big boulders everywhere and accuracy is the name of the game! Having nearly reached the halfway point they came to a long par three with water down the left side. His partners found the green with their tee shots, but Henrik's ball found the water.

On reaching the watery hazard, Henrik duly dropped a ball behind it and chipped on. By now, not only was it cold, but it had begun to drizzle, it really was quite miserable. But as he walked past the water he glanced in and stopped.

'Hey, wait a minute, there's my ball!' he said, 'I'll just get it out.'

Try as he would, he found it impossible to reach it from the bank, even using his longest club. Undeterred he took off one shoe and sock, rolled up his trouser leg and put his foot into the icy water, only to discover that he still couldn't reach the ball. (*It's funny, isn't it, how water clouds our perception of distance.*) Back on the bank off came the other shoe and sock, and the other trouser leg was pushed up to the knee.

He waded back in swirling his club in the water until it reached the ball, but try as he might, he just couldn't dislodge it (*the club golfer's nightmare!*). More wiggling, jiggling, prodding, but still it wouldn't move.

'Oh, to hell with it,' said Henrik, and with that he took a deep breath, ducked his head under the water and stared around. Pausing only to come up for air, he ducked under the surface again, groped in the murky depths and emerged clutching the ball.

Standing on the bank, blue with cold, and dripping from head to toe, he glanced at the white object in his hand.

'Hmmm, nice ball!' he said, 'But not mine!'

What did Palmer use? ...

One story which has done the rounds has featured more than one golfing legend and, more importantly, his caddy. The strongest link seems to be with Arnold Palmer so here's '*Tip's Tale*'.

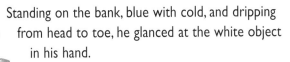

The story goes that a very good player, who was also a prolific hitter of a golf ball, was determined to realise an ambition to play Troon duplicating Palmer's 1962 Open Championship victory final round. All he needed was Palmer's caddy, Tip Anderson, and all the notes and measurements which they had used.

After much negotiation he managed to secure the Tip's services and it was agreed that the historic round would be recreated. All they had to do was to wait for the ideal conditions. At last the day arrived and they set off.

After 10 holes the golfer had matched Palmer stroke for stroke, absolutely level and to say he was delighted would be an understatement. The right clubs, the right line, it was perfect and he was becoming more and more excited. However, the par 4, dog-legged 11th at Troon is a very difficult hole, with gorse everywhere and the railway and wall hard against the green.

Undaunted the fellow stepped up to the tee and hit a superb drive into the perfect position. On reaching the ball, he turned to Tip and asked:

'What did Palmer use from here?'

Tip consulted the notes, '4 iron, sir,' he replied.

Taking his 4 iron the man hit an absolute sizzler right at the flag, but to his surprise it finished 50 yards short of the green.

'What the hell are you playing at?' he said angrily, 'You said Arnold took a 4 iron, I'm 50 yards short!'

'Yes,' said Tip, nodding his head, 'So was Arnold!'

A word of advice (part 1)...

On the way to the first tee juggle a ball to take your mind off the daunting task ahead ...

read on!...

A word of advice (part 2)...

As your juggling skills improve, add another ball, not only will this impress your playing partners but it will boost your confidence as well....

read on!....

What a beautiful day!

Rumour has it that the feudal code is still live and kicking. In a tale attributed to a golf club in Norfolk, we join a visitor arriving at the near-empty clubhouse.

Walking in to the bar he says, 'Good morning, nice day,' to the obligatory old member tucked down behind a copy of the *Daily Telegraph*.

No reply, just stony silence, undeterred he goes on:

'Hmmm, this is great!'

Still no reply. Stretching his arms and bouncing up and down on his heels he says, 'What a beautiful day! Do you know, it's my first visit here and I'm so looking forward to playing.'

Silence.

'Tell me, I've heard so much about the course. They say there's always a stiff, testing breeze, but there's not even a breath of wind outside. Do you think it'll be a problem later on?'

With that the old member grunts, puts down the paper, gets up from his chair and shuffles over to the bar and presses the bell. Soon the steward appears.

'Steward,' murmurs the old member, 'could you look after this fellow, I believe he wants conversation.'

A word of advice (part 3)...

Before long your new found skills will be the talk of the club, as by now you will have perfected the four ball 'one-hander' and will have progressed to ball juggling using your club ...

read on!...

What's your handicap?

During a business trip to Africa, a fanatical golfer decided to take a day off to play golf. Not knowing the area he asked at the hotel for directions to the nearest course. Discovering that it was in the heart of the jungle, he became very excited and quickly arranged for transport there.

He rushed in to the Pro Shop and requested a tee time. The Pro duly booked him in and at the same time asked him his handicap.

'If you really need to know?' said the man, 'It's 16, but I'm going to play on my own.'

The Pro apologised but insisted that it was absolutely imperative for the Club to know. With that he summoned a caddie from the back room and said:

'Can you go out with this gentleman? His handicap is 16.'

Rather surprised by the emphasis on his handicap, the businessman walked towards the first tee, the caddie carrying his bag on one shoulder and a large rifle on the other. Not wishing to appear overly concerned about this, the businessman stepped up to the first tee.

'Bwana, whatever you do, avoid those trees on the left,' said the caddie.

The man stepped up to the ball and 'thwack', he hooked it straight into the trees. Luckily he found it easily, but just as he was about to punch it out, 'BANG!', a rifle shot rang out and a snake fell dead from the tree above him.

'You're lucky I was here,' said the caddie, 'that's the most dangerous snake in Africa!'

Settling for a bogey 5, it was on to the next hole, a par 5, dog-leg left.

'Mind the bushes on the right, Bwana,' said the caddie.

Sure enough the tee shot sliced to the right and ended in the bushes. As the businessman went to pick up his ball there was another 'BANG!', the caddie's rifle had claimed another victim. A huge lion lay dead at his feet.

'Looks like I saved your life again!' he said, grinning from ear to ear.

The next hole was a par 3 with a sizeable lake in front of the green. No comment from the caddie this time and the businessman confidently hit his tee shot. It landed just short of the green, but rolled back to the edge of the water. The man wasn't worried, he had a shot, all he needed to do was to put one foot in the water to play it. As he prepared to chip a crocodile surfaced and bit off his right leg.

As he fell to the ground he shouted, 'Why didn't you shoot it?'

The caddie shrugged his shoulders, 'I'm sorry, sir,' he said. 'This hole is stroke index 17, you don't get a shot here!'

A word of warning!...

EDD ©1997

Be aware that greenkeepers often dislike juggling, to the extent that they place the tee markers directly in your path. By applying the basic rule of course management and planning your route you can easily avoid this hazard, and the two shot penalty for dropping your balls!...

Something to look forward to!

A highly enthusiastic golfer was introduced by a friend to a well-known and respected clairvoyant. They swiftly became friends, but the golfer was soon badgering his new found friend for news of the hereafter. He became increasingly desperate to know whether there was a golf course in Heaven. If there was, he wanted to know what sort of sand was in the bunkers? What was the par? How difficult was it? What was the pro shop like? and other questions like that.

Each time they met, or spoke on the phone, the subject came up until, at last, the clairvoyant agreed to tackle the subject at his next seance. Three weeks later the keen golfer, unable to contain himself any longer, contacted the clairvoyant who said:

'I've got some good news and some bad news.'

'Yes, yes!' said the golfer impatiently, 'What's the good news?'

'Well, I'm reliably informed that there is, without doubt, the most superb golf course in Heaven. Bermuda grass on the fairways, Penn Cross on the greens and the most exotic crushed marble in the bunkers. A fabulous clubhouse with every facility you've ever dreamed of and a pro shop where everything's free, you just choose what you want and take it away, it's amazing!'

The golfer was gobsmacked, 'Wow!' he said, 'So what's the bad news?'

'I've booked you a tee time for next Tuesday at 2 o'clock,' came the chirpy reply.

Have you booked?

'At last! At last! At last!' said the golfer, playing the round of his life, five under and two to play. Finishing the 16th he moves on to the par 5, 17th that has a large oak tree right in the middle of the fairway, just about driving distance. Teeing up his ball he hits a magnificent shot to the left side of the fairway.

When he reaches his ball he discovers a limb from the tree is hanging above it. A tough decision faces him, should he play it safe with a 7 iron or cast caution to the wind and blast a 3 wood? After a moment's thought he decides that nothing can go wrong because he's on a roll, so he gets out the 3 wood, takes a couple of practice swings and blasts into it.

The ball flies up straight up into the branch and rebounds onto his head, killing him instantly. The next thing he knows, he's at the Pearly Gates. St Peter is standing in front of him looking really flustered and is frantically flicking through the pages of a large book, he 'tuts', picks up a mobile phone and makes a couple of calls, and then checks the computer screen in front of him.

'I'm very sorry,' St Peter says, 'I can't find your name anywhere. How did you get here?'

'I got here in two!' the man replies.

heck distance from the ball, check width of stance and ball position, check aim and alignment, and weight distribution. Make a swing. Think knee flex, shaft on plane and weight transfer. Hit the ball and hold your finish!!

Right! That's the first shot out of the way. Only another ninety or so to go. And then there's the searching in the trees, the lining up of putts and calls of nature. Still let's enjoy it – it's supposed to be fun!! ... What's that it's been 4 hours already and we're only on the 3rd hole ...

– tell them we lost a ball!!

When the going gets slower!

During the quest for the elusive scorecard 'that dreams are made of', budding 'master' golfers may, unwittingly, lose track of time, locked uncontrollably in a web of indecision and kamikaze single-mindedness. Oblivious to all around, the intrepid players edge ever closer to the green, never quite on the fairway, plagued with 'bad bounces' and 'impossible lies', uttering cries of 'Why me?', 'Fore left!', 'Fore right!' and 'Did you see where it went?'

Always aware however of the social side of the game, great care is taken to generate conversation, usually in between shots and before and after putting out, followed by meaningful discussions of 'what might-have-beens' and 'if-onlys' in addition to scorecard completion before leaving each green.

With bags strategically placed at the furthest point away from the next tee, they wave apologetically at the following group as they amble leisurely back in front of the green and head for the tee, blissfully unaware that the players in front are six holes ahead and the light is fading fast. After numerous chats, 'calls of nature' in the trees, inch-by-inch searches of the undergrowth and thousands of practice swings, divots and duffs, the round eventually finishes with the comment

'Most enjoyable, never got held up once! ... Same time next week?'

Back on the course chaos reigns, with groups queuing five deep on each tee. Tempers flare, clubs fly, scores soar and the light fails!

The Ranger

A thankless job, but someone's got to do it! Feared, respected, kind and considerate, never around when you need them, but always around when you don't!

FOUR!

During a Society Day, the last fourball had lost two holes on the group in front and were making their way from the halfway hut to the 10th tee. As they arrived the course ranger pulled up in his buggy and asked the group, in view of their slow play, if his passenger could play through.

He went on to reassure them that the man was not only a good player, but an extremely long hitter and certainly wouldn't hold them up. At the same time he felt it prudent to point out that the man was both deaf and dumb.

The fourball, after a brief discussion amongst themselves, declined the ranger's request stressing that, having paid their money, they could play at whatever pace they wanted and in any case they were all long hitters as well!

So having hit their tee shots the fourball set off down the fairway and in turn took their second shots. The longest hitter out of the four had put his second shot 10 feet from the flag and was busy boasting to his playing partners about his expertise when a ball from the tee rapped him on the back of the neck.

He turned angrily round to see, way back on the tee, the animated figure of the deaf and dumb man, frantically waving four fingers in the air!

Ouch!!

Two ladies, playing in a knockout competition, were teeing off on the 4th.

The first lady hit a slight fade and ended in the middle of the fairway. The second hit a block which hurtled at alarming speed towards a men's fourball on the next fairway. In open-mouthed horror they watched as the ball hit one of the group and he collapsed in a heap on the floor clutching his groin, before either could even think about shouting 'fore!' They rushed over to the stricken man, and the woman whose ball had gone off line, said, 'I'm ever so sorry, please let me help. I'm a physiotherapist and I'm sure I can relieve your pain, if you'll let me.'

The man, still clutching his hands to his groin, was obviously embarrassed by the fuss, but was still doubled up in pain.

'Um, ahhh, errhh, no it's all right, I'll be OK in a minute,' he replied, quite obviously in distress.

But the woman persisted, and, finally, he agreed that she could help. Slowly and carefully she moved his hands to the side and loosened his trousers. She put her hands inside and began to massage.

'Does that feel any better?' she said.

'That feels great,' he replied, 'but my thumb still hurts like hell!'

Baby came too

Hugh Lewis was the pro at Altrincham Golf Club and the 8th green there was just by the pro shop window. One day he was in the shop, when somebody said:

'Hugh, Hugh! Quick! Look out there.'

Hugh looked out and could see a fellow lining up a six or seven-foot putt from all angles. Near him, standing right in the middle of the green, was a very attractive woman in high-heeled boots with, beside her, a huge pram, which she was jiggling up and down.

Horrified, Hugh rushed out, went up to the chap and started to reason with him. Keeping his back to the woman, and speaking as quietly as possible, he said:

'I'm sorry, but we really can't have this. I mean, it's not as if she's going round the edge of the green, she's right in the middle wearing stiletto heels and, as if that's not enough, she's got that great big pram!'

The golfer replied with a desperate look on his face.

'I know she shouldn't, but she won't let me out of the house unless she comes with me. So if she doesn't come, I don't get a game of golf at all.'

Poor Hugh was gobsmacked, he really didn't know what to say and he felt genuinely sorry for the chap. As he turned away, he looked once more at the pram and noticed that, instead of using a bag, the chap was laying his clubs across it and underneath was a basket with several golf balls and some golf tees.

Back in the pro shop, in a moment of lunatic inspiration, Hugh wondered perhaps if there wasn't room on the golfing market for such a special pram, on which you could rest your clubs and other golfing gear. Sanity, alas, returned and he never did anything about it, turning a blind eye to the pram and the high-heeled boots.

(Well, nearly a blind eye to the boots !)

69

It's supposed to be fun!

It's such a silly game. All games are silly, arguably, but golf, if you look at it dispassionately, does go to such extremes. There's so much to think about, and eighteen holes to the average golfer never seems long enough to remember, let alone implement, all the subtleties of the game.

Perhaps we can help ...

Junior Golf

losely similar to the adult game, but without the fears or inhibitions. Considered a threat in many clubs and often penalised with time restrictions for play, the junior golfer successfully demonstrates how the game should be played at all levels. With the very best in modern technology filling their lightweight carry-bags junior golfers never cease to amaze, not least because they all believe they have the same name!

They're so much bigger nowadays ...

Never work with animals and children they say in showbusiness, but I'm happy to say the same 'rules' don't apply to golf. I'm not convinced about the animals, but children and golf, or juniors as we know them, are a more than welcome asset to the game. I don't know whether it's my imagination, but they really do seem to be making them all so much bigger nowadays. Don't they?

'I wish I'd taken it up at that age,' is the cry round the clubhouse, as golfers, old and older, marvel at the aptitude and achievements of their younger counterparts.

With youthful exuberance and dedicated practise the would-be junior golfer quickly masters the fundamentals and is soon regularly making contact with the ball. In no time at all, with confidence high, it's time for the first junior competition, where the only difficulty is with butterflies on the first tee. In the blink of an eye the handicap comes tumbling down, the confidence grows further, junior trophies fill the mantelpiece and adult competitions beckon. It's an easy game!

A word of caution though , Edd's sixteen year old son Andrew, a two-handicapper, warns that success can have its drawbacks and tells of a junior golfing ailment called 'Golfer's Nipple'. It apparently only affects lower handicap juniors wearing county or club team shirts, when the reverse side of the embroidered logos causes soreness of the nipples, making even the simplest of swings painful. But don't worry, you don't need to take tablets or medicines to effect a cure, as the simple wearing of a T-shirt underneath will avoid unnecessary discomfort.

Sore nipples aside, there really is a wealth of talent out there and, with the help of the current initiatives for junior recruitment, coaching and development, long may there continue to be.

It's odd to think though that, despite all this, there is still resistance in some quarters to the playing aspirations of youngsters at club level, with all sorts of restrictions being placed on when they can, or can't play, regardless of ability.

What do I do?

When your partner, or opponent, is about to play a stroke, be quiet, stand still and don't stand too close or ahead of the ball, you might get hurt!

Always 'play without delay', but, from a safety point of view, do not play until the group in front is out of range, because it's very rare that body armour and hard hats are being worn! If you can't find your ball, even though you're allowed five minutes to look for it, think about the group behind and let them through as soon as you realise that your search is going to take time. It's worth remembering that a single (*that doesn't mean not married!*) player has no standing on the course, so if you're playing alone you will be expected to give way to a match of any kind.

While on the course it's worth thinking about what you might leave behind after you've taken your shot, or when you're leaving the green. So try not to wreak havoc with your practice swing, particularly on the tees and don't forget to replace your divots on the fairways, taking the trouble to heel them back in. Don't replace a divot made on the tee, as the teeing ground should always be firm under foot.

Always leave bunkers as you would wish to find them and never leave them by walking up the face. Most times you can use a nearby rake but, if you can't find one, use a club or your foot to smooth the sand after you've played your shot. Don't forget if you're using a trolley, look out for the signs which tell you where you can, and can't, go when nearing greens or bunkers.

Once on the greens, repair your pitch-marks (and others you might find) either before you putt or before you leave the green. It doesn't take a lifetime and the quality of the greens will definitely improve, particularly if everyone else does it as well. While you're there, try not to lean on your putter or use it as a prop when taking your ball out of the hole, as this can damage the putting surface.

The Ball

There is something magical about being able to hit the ball a lot further than anyone else, like Tiger Woods or John Daly. Most club golfers want to do likewise, but few of them seem to realise the advantages, or disadvantages, of using a golf ball suited to their style of play.

Ball manufacturers' products range in compression from 100, which is hard, to 90, which is a little softer, and there are some even softer still at 80 compression. Its worth noting that if you don't hit the ball as far as you would like, it may be that you're using a ball which is too hard for you.

Unfortunately the choice doesn't end there. The next decision centres around the ball's construction, should it be two piece or three piece? As a rule of thumb, the two piece ball will last longer and not cut so easily as the traditional three-piece 'wound'. Then there's the choice of high trajectory, low trajectory,

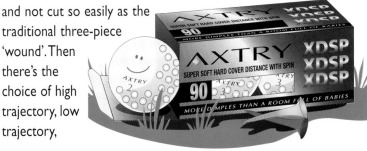

distance, high spin, low spin and the promise of much more. Think about it, golf balls are expensive and although a bargain is a bargain, take just a little bit of trouble to find a ball that suits *your* game, on the tee, on the fairway and on the green.

Give yourself an opportunity to experiment with different types before committing yourself to bulk purchase. Don't be afraid to ask for advice, your pro will be only too pleased to help and the correct choice will almost certainly knock shots off your game and might even seriously reduce your handicap.

Follow the line

Choice of ball certainly affects the short game, nowhere more so than on the greens. When on the course prepare yourself for the putting challenge ahead as you approach the green, by looking to see whether it slopes to the left or right, back to front, or whatever. If you have to chip your ball on to the putting surface, the way it rolls across the green will give a good clue to the contours and, since every putt requires distance and direction, the contours of the green determine both the line and weight your putt will need.

Persuading yourself that every putt is straight will certainly help your confidence and, once you have decided the line the putt should take, just hit the ball straight along that line, and allow the contours to take the ball to the hole. One of the very best ways to help yourself to develop the confidence to do this is to pick a spot 12 inches in front of the ball, and putt over this mark. Try it, it'll work wonders for you!

The Three Putt

Dedication to technique and purposeful practise can achieve perfection in this much maligned skill. Featured extensively by both professionals and club golfers alike, it is ideally suited to any pace of green both home and abroad.

The ideal complement to the duffed or thinned chip and the seven iron pitch-and-run shank.

Is it my ball?

It's important during play that you should be able to identify your ball and, although all golf balls are marked with a number and a brand name, you should always put your own personal identification mark on yours. With a felt pen draw a series of dots, or draw faces, or your initials – it's up to you.

Having marked it appropriately, you should always ensure that it is *your* ball before playing it, but, if it is in a hazard and you can't identify it without handling it, play the ball out and identify it afterwards. If you've played the wrong ball, there's no penalty and the stroke is not counted. However, if your ball is in a hazard and you lift or rotate it in order to make an identification, it will cost you a penalty stroke.

You can mark, lift and identify your ball anywhere, except when it's in a hazard. But be careful, you can only clean it as far as is necessary to identify it. However, make sure you don't touch it for identification until you've told your fellow competitor, opponent or marker, so that he/she can have the opportunity to watch you mark, lift, identify and then replace it in the same place. There's a one stroke penalty if you don't do this.

If your ball is in long grass, carefully touch or move only as much of the grass as is necessary to make identification, but be careful, if you improve the lie of your ball there's a penalty. In Match Play it's loss of the hole and in Stroke Play it's a hefty two strokes!

The Shank!...

EDD ©1997

Used extensively by golfers of all abilities, the shank relies heavily on an out-to-in swing path. Perfect contact close to the hosel makes the ball fly off sharply to the right, which in tight matchplay situations can successfully eliminate the opposition.

Practice of this shot should not be undertaken on the range!!...

When the squiggly bit takes over

The Shank (socket or pipe) is a dreadful affliction which can strike even the best of players without warning. It's what happens when you strike a golf ball, not with the face of the club, but with the hosel or socket of the clubhead (the squiggly bit where the shaft joins the clubhead). The ball flies off furiously at right angles, completely out of control. Next to the air shot (a complete miss) it is considered the most embarrassing thing that can happen to a golfer.

One person who did it often, if not regularly, was Dai Rees, five times Ryder Cup captain – and a winning one at that. The experts maintained that this was because Dai had a loose grip, a two-handed baseball grip with the left hand very much underneath, showing no knuckles at all. It was socketing, I seem to remember, which cost him an Open Championship at Troon back in the fifties. Dai was seriously in contention when on the 12th, after a good drive down the fairway, he shanked into a bunker, took six or seven, and that ended his challenge.

As far as I can remember I've only had three, two of them were in bunkers, with the clubface laid open so much that I simply presented the hosel to the ball. The other time, however, was on a practice ground with about 20 people looking on. I was poncing about as usual, taking deep breaths and looking terribly smart. I whipped a 9-iron out of the bag, one swish, one swing and bang! Away she went straight out of the pipe, leaving an embarrassed Alliss, pretending I had been distracted by something or other!

Although it is not something that can be cured in a couple of simple sentences, we can say that an early symptom is the pulled shot, when the ball flies straight left, with the face of the club pointing left and the divot pointing left. To be honest, it has many causes. Whether it is insufficient shoulder turn, static legs, head too much over the ball at address or starting the downswing with the right shoulder, the ultimate reason for shanking is that the swing path has gone outside the line (outside the proper swing plane), with the clubface pulled across the ball.

The shank is invariably worse with short iron shots and pitching clubs and often it happens because you are concentrating on pitching over a bunker or to a precise spot on the green, nervously thinking more about the destination of the ball, rather than the execution of the swing. One immediate treatment for this virus is to raise the head and upper body at address and stand tall.

Taking a more closed stance will also help counter the affliction, but most of all you need to concentrate on swinging the clubhead instead of hitting at the ball, good advice really for every single shot in golf.

Beat the clock!

Slow play is one of the curses of modern golf and many say it's because members lack the discipline instilled by those wonderful old, retired wing commanders and colonels who were club secretaries years ago. Whatever the cause, it's hard to believe that some players still don't take the simple precaution of having a spare ball in their pocket, spending endless time searching aimlessly in the rough and then walking back 30, 40 or 50 yards to their golf bag to get another. Others never even have a tee peg in their pockets and, predictably, when it's their turn to play, the glove isn't on either. Have you ever thought about the amount of time wasted taking a glove from your back pocket, squeezing your fingers into it, flexing them, fastening the glove, then stepping up to the ball only to find you don't have a tee peg handy. That's 20, 30 or may be even 40 seconds wasted, and if this happens on every hole, with every shot, and you're playing fourball, the round could be an hour or an hour and a half longer than it should have been – makes you think, doesn't it?

The Rules of Golf say, 'In the interests of all, players should play without undue delay.' Obviously the weather and other golfers on the course, in varying permutations and varieties, can affect the general pace, but rounds of three and a half hours or less should be well within the reach of all golfers, with a modicum of common sense and a little forethought.

Firstly, try to make sure everyone in your group follows the flight of each ball, at least then you'll know where to look in the rough or the trees. Hit a provisional ball (the one in your pocket!) if you think yours might have gone out of bounds or irretrievably into the woods. Remember, the rules say that you have five minutes to find such a ball, but that doesn't mean that you have to make the people playing behind wait that long. Be considerate, let them through if the hole ahead is clear, that way play keeps moving and everyone's happy.

Think about your next shot as you approach your ball, don't wait until you reach it. Check the route to the next tee when nearing the green and be sure to leave your bag or trolley at the tee side of the green.

Once on the green the player furthest from the hole plays first, and if that's not you, then you have a chance to study your line and can be ready to putt when your turn comes. When you've all finished putting, replace the flagstick and go straight to the next tee. Remember, it's not the place to add up your score, fill in your scorecard or discuss the economy.

The irony is that Bobby Locke, the great South African Champion, was constantly castigated for playing slowly during his illustrious career. He would take two and three quarter hours, perhaps two hours 50 minutes, to play a round. Admittedly that was for two-ball matches, but he was averaging 45 minutes quicker than the briskest of rounds today, and he had to fight through crowds of spectators in between shots!

Hold your finish!....

... but not for too long!

Danger, Golf in Progress!

As a spectator sport, golf has developed almost beyond recognition during the past thirty-odd years. With tented villages now double glazed and giant video screens showing play, encouragement to watch is now greater than ever.

The vast majority of people who attend are, if not experienced golfers, knowledgeable about the sport and its intricacies, and highly appreciative of the playing skills demonstrated.

With this high level of understanding and appreciation of the finer points, it seems hard to believe that a degree of naivety exists on the spectator 'walkways'. Cast your eyes round the crowds at any major championship or tournament and see what happens between shots.

Silently they surround the tees, watching in admiration, perfectly still, apart from the odd foot shuffle. But all too often, having seen their hero's shot, they scurry off down the walkways to the next vantage point not waiting for the other competitors' shots, comfortable with the fact that it's very difficult for a golf ball to cross over the rope that keeps the crowds off the fairways!

DANGER GOLF IN PROGRESS

The Spectator Slide

A modern day phenomenon from the spectators' growing achievement portfolio appears to be caused by over-enthusiastic haste, rather than measured speed and is often witnessed on undulating courses which are wet under foot.

Edd tells of a visit to the Oxfordshire, Thame, for the Benson & Hedges International in 1998, when the first round was delayed by thunderstorms and torrential rain. When play eventually began, five and a half hours late, it was still raining and spectators thronged around the starting tees, bedecked resplendently in stunning white, voluminous Slazenger PVC ponchos (*eat your heart out Clint Eastwood*).

A large section of the crowd around the 10th tee broke away to follow the group in which Lee Westwood, Jose Maria Olazabal and Constantino Rocca were playing. Obviously spurred

on by the excitement of the scintillating golf and a hell-bent desire to reach a vantage point before anyone else, the scene was reminiscent of a cross-country race.

However, in the hurry to gain the next vantage point, it became increasingly evident that perhaps it might have been better to wear sensible shoes. With the rain having now stopped, ponchos had now been removed and light colour clothing revealed.

And then it happened! Ooops! Bodies were dropping, or rather slipping, like nine-pins. With uncanny regularity people in front, and behind, lost their footing on the muddied grass. More and more brown stripes appeared down the legs of trousers as their occupants tumbled. Throughout the round, the smooth passage of spectators was punctuated frequently by their slippery demise, while the ever-increasing presence of thick brown stripes threatened to make a serious fashion statement.

So what's the point of this diatribe, you may say. Well the strange thing is that, without exception, every brown, muddy stripe featured only on the right hand side! It would be interesting to know what the odds on that happening are, or do we, due to some freak of nature, always fall on the right side?

Edd says 'No!' He went back to the Oxfordshire this year for the same tournament. The weather was considerably better, although, under foot, it was still pretty damp. Guess what? No, you're wrong! This time, although not in such vast numbers, the brown stripes were predominantly left-sided, apart from one man who had managed to stripe his right arm and his left leg.

Have you noticed anything similar? (*Answers on a postcard, please!*)

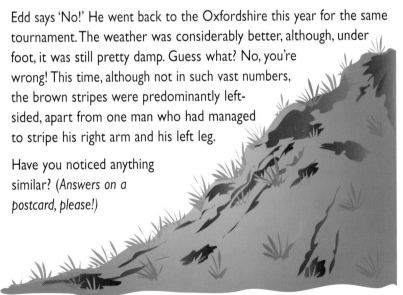

Around the **RULES**

The Rules of Golf are all too often considered to be a miserable catalogue of penalties, with sadistic punishment for errant play.

Put the smile back in your game with a smidgen of understanding and a touch of common sense you can make the rules work for you.

You might even enjoy using them! ...

The Rules of Golf, believe it or not, total only 34 in number. However, they carry with them definitions and numerous appendices that make the whole thing run to about 100 pages. At first glance, or even at second, third, fourth, fifth, sixth, seventh or more glances they can appear both restrictive and intimidating.

For the average society, fair weather or club golfer they serve to complicate and frustrate the continual battle for supremacy over the disobedient antics of the small white ball. Rumour has it that there are players who actually enjoy the heated exchanges that arise in both casual and competitive play, but the stressful uncertainty of such arguments and doubtful decisions can severely hinder enjoyment and will almost certainly increase blood pressure and possibly accelerate hair loss.

'Better the devil you know,' they say, and how right they are!

Join us on a simplified tour of some of the rules and procedures, and discover how they can benefit your game and possibly your health!

Unplayable Lie

The player may declare his ball unplayable at any place on the course except when the ball lies in or touches a water hazard. The player is the sole judge as to whether his ball is unplayable. If the player deems his ball to be unplayable, under penalty of one stroke, he may:

a) play a ball as nearly as possible at the spot from which the original ball was played;

b) drop a ball within two clublengths of the spot where the ball lay (not nearer the hole);

or

c) drop a ball behind the point where the ball lay, keeping that point directly between the hole and the spot on which the ball is dropped, with no limit to how far behind that point the ball may be dropped. If the unplayable ball is in a bunker, the player may proceed as above except that under clauses (b) or (c) it must be dropped in the bunker.

Ground under repair

Any portion of the course marked GUR by the committee. It includes material piled for removal, and any hole made by a greenkeeper, even if not so marked. Stakes and lines defining ground under repair are included in such ground. The player may lift and drop the ball without penalty at a point on the course nearest to where the ball lay, provided it is not nearer the hole, not interfered with by the ground under repair and not in a hazard or on a putting green.

Lifting and dropping a ball

These procedures are probably the most misapplied in the game. When a ball has to be lifted under a rule which means it will be replaced, its position must be marked before it is lifted. If this is not done, there is a penalty of one stroke and the ball should be replaced. If the ball or the marker are accidentally moved in the process of lifting or marking, there is no penalty. The ball or ball-marker should be replaced.

When dropping a ball under the rules the player should stand erect, holding the ball at arm's length and shoulder height and then dropping it. If it touches the player, his partner, or their caddies or equipment before or after it touches part of the course, it must be re-dropped, without penalty. A dropped ball shall also be re-dropped without penalty if it:

i) rolls into a hazard

ii) rolls out of a hazard

iii) rolls on to a putting green

iv) rolls out of bounds

v) rolls to a position where there is interference by the condition from which relief was taken

vi) comes to rest more than two clublengths from where it first struck part of the course

vii) rolls and comes to rest nearer the hole than its original position.

Winter Rules

As far as the Rules of Golf are concerned, there is no such thing. The words do not appear in the rules. Neither, incidentally, does the word 'fairway', which will surprise lots of people. However the club committee can make a temporary local rule to cover abnormal conditions. and this they call 'winter rules'. The temporary rule allows you to roll the ball over or lift and place it into a better lie, usually within six inches of where it lay. You're also allowed to clean it. All this might sound a bit complicated, but it is designed to 'protect the course, and promote fair and pleasant play'.

Outside agency

Contrary to public opinion, an 'outside agency' is not a place where you arrange a date or find a job, but something which may interfere with your golf ball during play. It is something, or someone, that is not part of the match or, in stroke play, not part of the competitors side. Human outside agencies can include referees, markers, observers, ball spotters (forecaddies), or even spectators. At the same time a bird or an animal which might disturb the ball can also be an outside agency, but neither wind nor water are outside agencies.

It's a relief to know! ...

So, having decided to take a penalty drop, how do you go about it when you decide to:

'Go back as far as you like'

Well, the penalty for this procedure is one stroke. First draw an imaginary line direct from the hole to a spot on which you wish to drop the ball, this line *must* cross the exact position of where your unplayable ball lay (*called the reference point*). Your penalty drop should only be made along this imaginary line and should never be nearer to the hole.

If your ball has gone into a water/lateral water hazard, then your *reference point* is where the ball last crossed the margin of the water hazard, *not* where the ball came finished in the hazard. If your ball crosses a water hazard *twice* in one shot, then your *reference point* is where it *last* crossed the margin of the hazard.

One club or two? ....

Isn't it funny how the old memory fails when the question '*One club-length or two?*' is asked. If you have difficulty in remembering the answer to this, try this simple adage: **'one** *club-length is* **free; two** *club-lengths* **you have to pay for!**' Sometimes, however, some Clubs allow a drop without penalty within two club-lengths, *or even more*, always check the Local Rules on the score card.

Stroke-and-distance ....

If your ball is lost or out of bounds, you have no choice but to take a stroke-and-distance penalty. All very well I hear you say, but what does it really mean?

It's simple really, all it means is that you play your next stroke from where you played the last stroke, adding a penalty stroke to your score. If it was your tee shot, you play the next stroke from the tee (*three off the tee*), teeing the ball up again. When you take a stroke-and-distance penalty through the green (*on the course*), in a bunker, or in a water/lateral water hazard, you 'drop' a ball on or as near as possible to the spot

On the course...

Pars, birdies, eagles, bogeys, double-bogeys, out-of-bounds, in the water, in the trees, in the rough, in the bunkers. Three putts, four putts, duffed chips, thins, hooks, slices, blocks, pushes, duffs, shanks and lost balls.

So much to look forward to! . . . .

EDD © 1999

Something to smile about!

Throughout the world, a plethora of 'on the course' and 'off the course' advice flows freely amongst amateur golfers, eager to correct the mistakes of others while remaining oblivious to their own. Apart from over complicating the game and its many challenges, such advice frequently creates intense mental and physical pressures for the recipients, substituting stress and frustration for relaxation and enjoyment. All too easily the fun side of the game is forgotten and hitherto pleasant personalities and smiling faces are sadly left behind in the locker room.

Lessons from the pro, instructional videos and books compete to improve our playing skills, but no one takes time to tell us that there will also be plenty of opportunities to look silly and feel stupid or that there might actually be something to smile about both in play and practice.

read on . . .

In search of perfection

Countless hours spent painstakingly perfecting the subtleties of the game such as the 'golfer's lean', 'the duff', the 'air shot', the 'thinned chip' and the 'skied drive', whilst attempting to empty bucket after bucket of balls faster than everyone else on the range!

... the search goes on ...

Try not to overdo the backswing!...

... and on ...

On the range!

Fade, draw, slice, hook, pull, shank, push, pull hook, top, scuff, air shot, duck hook, thin, in-to-out, out-to-in, steep swing, flat swing. Strong grip, weak grip, weight forward, weight back, open stance, closed stance, tight grip, loose grip...

... and I've still got sixteen balls left !!!

The Practice Swing

EDD ©1997

The ultimate combination of athleticism, rhythm and timing, unhindered by swing thoughts, tension or stress. A poetical blur in motion. Rarely reproduced on or off the course when ball introduction is implemented!...

The tee!....

Described by many as the modern day, outdoor equivalent to a torture chamber. Success or failure in a split second with eighteen (or more) opportunities to discover, and then demonstrate, your innermost 'animal' self to your playing partners, whilst simultaneously agonising with swing thoughts better suited to hours of careful deliberation.

EDD © 1999

... are you ready?

Technology takes over!

As manufacturers battle for sweet spot supremacy and cries of 'Mine's bigger and goes further than yours!' replace the more traditional cry of 'Fore!'

The First Tee!...

Strategically placed in full view of the clubhouse, the first tee provides the perfect setting for stress, anxiety and mild palpitations. The ultimate challenge of mind over matter, with an early opportunity to demonstrate the animal-like, aggressive side of your nature, whilst struggling with involuntary muscle twitching and over-active butterflies!...   ...F-F-F-Fore!!...

The Skied Drive!

A lthough often viewed as a bad shot, the skied drive, once perfected, can be used extensively for familiarising a golf ball with the course and its layout. Dedicated practice can ensure that the balance between strength of grip, angle of attack and tee height will maximise the ball's view of the course.

Ideally suited to the higher handicapper using high trajectory, two-piece distance balls!

Nothing to worry about!

Par 5, 575 yards, Stroke Index 1. Out of bounds right and left, 200 yard carry over thick heather off tee. Dog leg left, beware large oak tree centre of fairway. Blind 3rd shot 150 yards over water to elevated green. Out of bounds behind green, bunkers left, right and in front.

Pro's tip: 'Enjoy the scenery!'...

Just like the Pros!...

Fade, draw – you name it, we'll play it!....

... well almost! ...

The Fade!

*O*nly affects humans and animals. Warn your playing partners if you're likely to hit one. Hit too many and you might disappear completely!!...

The Draw!

G uaranteed to put the colour back in your cheeks!
The perfect complement to the fade, ideally
played at the earliest possible opportunity!!...

The Air Shot

EDD © 1997

Difficult to play consistently well but used extensively by amateurs for both social golf and club competitions. Unlike the missed duff or top, the perfect air shot relies exclusively on swingspeed, timing and flawless technique to achieve maximum absence of impact.

The Lob Shot...

EDD © 1997

The 'creme de la creme' of approach shots, played to perfection by professionals and talented amateurs alike, but viewed with fear and trepidation by most other players. To overcome this the technique of 'sans club' is sometimes used, with the affected player opting for hand assisted ball projection ...

(but only when their playing partners are looking the other way!)...

The Sandcastle Shot!...

When faced with a plugged lie in a sandcastle left over from a corporate day's golf, many players rush angrily into the bunker without taking time to think about the shot that faces them. In their haste to play the ball they often discover that, for once, the ever elusive rake is exactly where it should be!

The Almost Birdie!

EDD © 1999

The delicate, but involuntary, art of missing the hole by the smallest possible margin in order to set up a return putt (or two) guaranteed to test the technique and set the pulse racing!

A little something...

... for the mantelpiece! ...

The ultimate goal! ...

Although it's nice just to take part, it's even better to take home a trophy. However, it's always advisable to check out the size of the prizes first, just in case winning would involve reinforcing the mantlepiece, raising the ceiling or building an extension!

Still, the victory speech can be fun!

Nearly, but not quite! ...

Although winning's nice, the runner-up's spot does have its advantages. As the trophy's not so big you won't need to reinforce the mantlepiece, raise the ceiling or build an extension to accommodate it! ...

... and you don't have to make a speech!

Nearest the Pin...

A competition within a competition, where skill, judgement, club selection, natural golfing ability and accuracy are more than often replaced by a lucky bounce (or two, or even three or four)!

The Longest Drive...

Slice, hook, pull, shank, push, top, scuff,
air shot, thin, fat! Then it happened. Wallop!
– middle of the fairway (well nearly) and
very long, well longer than anyone else.
What a swing, absolute
poetry in motion!

Wish I could
remember
how I did it!

A great round!...

T wo birdies, an eagle, a handbag, two rabbits, four
trees and a telegraph pole, and I've still got the
ball I started off with!

And finally...

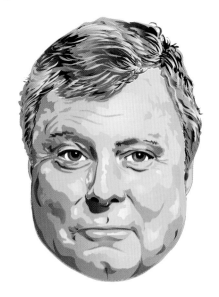

'Golf is one of the finest games in the
world. Because of its unique handicapping
system it's a game between equals. You can
start playing when quite young or you can
take it up when you are old. If you want
fresh air and exercise, stimulation and
challenge, relaxation and pleasure,
my advice is – *play golf.*'

There have been many quotable quotes by those associated with
golf over the years. Inspirational gems to fire the imagination, words
of wisdom to enrich understanding and humorous asides to increase
enjoyment. On the following pages you'll find some of the best.

Quotes to quote

'Put the main control where it belongs, into the hands, wrists and arms. Keep the body as relaxed as possible and give the idea a chance,' *Grantland Rice*

'One of the greatest menaces to good driving for the average golfer is that he is never satisfied with the length he gets from a well-hit ball.' *Tommy Armour*

'No one ever swings too slowly. Over-effort is the cause of the average golfer's trouble.' *Bobby Jones*

'Waiting for the clubhead to come through is one of the most difficult things we do in golf.' *H.B. Martin*

'Golf is a game played on a five inch course between the ears.' *Bobby Jones*

'It'll take three damn good shots to get up in two today.' *Old caddie's saying*

'In golf, the ball usually lies poorly and the player well.' *Anon*

'Golf is not a funeral, although both can be very sad affairs.'
Bernard Darwin

'A man who can putt is a match for anyone.'
Willie Park Senior

'My ideal in life is to read a lot, write a little, play plenty of golf, and have nothing to worry about.' *A.J. Balfour*

'It's better to smash your clubs than lose your temper.'
A.J. Balfour

'What a round! It wasn't just replacing the turf, more like returfing the place.' *Anon*

'I've never played a perfect 18 holes, there's no such thing.' *Walter Hagen*

'How well you play golf depends on how well you control that left hand of yours.'
Tommy Armour

'Play the shot you can play best, not the shot that would look best if you could pull it off.' *Harvey Penick*

'I say, are those your old school colours or your own unfortunate choice?' *Bernard Darwin* (to the wearer of an garishly bright outfit at St Andrews)

'I want a ruling. I want to know which club to hit this guy with.' *Hubert Green* (after a television buggy had run over his ball)

'You will look like holiday-makers if we allow you to wear shorts.' *John Paramour* (about the Johnny Walker Golf World Championships, held in 90° temperatures in Jamaica)

'See if you can hit three shots in a row on the practice range, without ever taking your hands off the handle or moving your fingers in any way. If you can do this your grip is solid and you can use a glove all summer without wearing a hole in it.'
Harvey Penick.

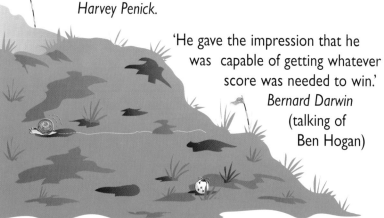

'He gave the impression that he was capable of getting whatever score was needed to win.'
Bernard Darwin
(talking of
Ben Hogan)

'Every day I try to tell myself this is going to be fun today.

I try to put myself in a great frame of mind before I go out, then I screw it up with the first shot.'

Johnny Miller

ENJOY YOUR GOLF

First published in 1999 by
André Deutsch Ltd
76 Dean Street
London W1V 5HA
www.vci.co.uk

A catalogue record for this book is available from the British Library

ISBN 0 233 99750 4

Printed and bound in Italy by G.E.P. S.p.A

1 3 5 7 9 10 8 6 4 2